POEMS

David Tomas Martinez

Sarabande  Books

LOUISVILLE, KENTUCKY

FIRST EDITION

Managing Editor
Sarabande Books, Inc.
2234 Dundee Road, Suite 200
Louisville, KY 40205

Library of Congress Cataloging-in-Publication Data

Martinez, David Tomas, 1976–
[Poems. Selections]
HUSTLE : Poems / David Tomas Martinez.—First Edition.
    pages cm
Includes bibliographical references and index.
ISBN 978-1-936747-77-1 (paperback : acid-free paper)
I. Title.
PS3613.A786424H87 2014
811'.6—dc23
                    2013031026

Cover art: Tattoo design by Brian Romero.

Cover and interior layout by Kirkby Gann Tittle.

Manufactured in Canada.

This book is printed on acid-free paper.

Sarabande Books is a nonprofit literary organization.

This project is supported in part by an award from the National Endowment for the Arts.

The Kentucky Arts Council, the state arts agency, supports Sarabande Books with state tax dollars and federal funding from the National Endowment for the Arts.

For Glover, Sandra, and Tony
For Brittney

CONTENTS

On Palomar Mountain   1

I.

Calaveras   5

II.

To The Young   27
Shed   29
Sabbath Fe Minus   32
California Penal Code 266   35
In Chicano Park   37
The Only Mexican   39
Innominatus   41

III.

Motion and Rest   47
Small Discoveries   51
The Sofa King   53
Apotropaic   54
The Cost of it All   56
Rebecca's Use   57
Coveralls   60

IV.

Forgetting Willie James Jones   65
Of Mockingbirds   80
Scientifically Speaking   82
This Bird Chest Holds a Bird's Heart   83
They Say I Teach English, I Say   85
A Sunday March   88
The Mechanics of Men   90

Notes   *93*
Acknowledgments   *95*
The Author   *97*

ON PALOMAR MOUNTAIN

The dark peoples with things:

for keys, coins, pencils
and pens our pockets grieve.

No street lights or signs,
no liquor stores or bars,
only a lighter for a flashlight,

and the same-faced trees,
similar-armed stones
and crooked bushes
staring back at me.

There is no path in the woods for a boy from the city.

I would have set fire to get off this wilderness
but Palomar is no El Camino in an empty lot,

the plastic dripping from the dash
and the paint bubbling like a toad's throat.

If mountains were old pieces of furniture,
I would have lit the fabric and danced.

If mountains were abandoned crack houses,
I would have opened their meanings with flame,

if that would have let the wind and trees lead my eyes
or shown me the moon's tip-toe on the moss—

as you effect my hand,
as we walk into the side of a Sunday night.

I

CALAVERAS

1.

A car wants to be stolen,
as the night desires to be revved,

will leave a door unlocked,
a key in the wheel well

or designedly dropped from a visor.

A window will always wink,
to be broken by bits of spark plug
or jimmied down the glass.

This is mine.
Where is the window to break
in your life?

In a backyard off the 94, I demonstrate on the moon
how a dent pulled ignition and a toothbrush for a turned key
easily swoon the inner workings of a Ford.

Push the dent puller in,
turn the triangle, burrow the screw,
and metallic light falls in twirled shavings.

Before I snap the weight I say
nobody gets caught with this,

not because this is a felony,
we speak of prison inevitably,
as likely as sweeps and raids,

as common as falling.
Prison, for us,
taxes and deaths.

Nobody gets caught with this
because I took it from my grandfather's tools.
. . .

To shoot someone we needed a gun;
Albert said he could get a pistol but we needed a car.

That's how, at midnight, on a Tuesday,
we strolled down the street with a dent puller

trying to murder a man.

Not wanting to steal a car
from our neighborhood,

we take alleys we shouldn't,
until cops chase us across
eight lanes of freeway and backyards.

To get away, I ran in a canyon
and a field of cactus.

The needles ripped my clothes,
left spiked fruit behind my knee;

with a knife wet under a garden hose,
I cut away skin and spines.

With arms around my boys' shoulders
we walk home, but only I see god.

It was the Lord from his La Jollan gates,
the big white man in the sky hollered at me.

In pale distance and omniscient beard,
in sky clouded with open azure:

No murder this night for you,
nor any night for you,

only a hot bath and plate of papas fritas
from a grandmother's hands

and four hours of needles
shooting from the skin

and holding the faucet like a gun.

2.

Yes, families are supposed to be circuses.
Accept it, and accept that the acrobat's taffy
of satin will twirl, and the bears in tutus will spin

over the exposes in the warped wood
and cracks in the waxy linoleum,
all the while your grandfather will yell

You no like it, go in the canyon and eat tomatoes.

Avoid his boots from under the Mercury Marquis.
Accept your aunt, the invisible lady, naked in the yard,
mustached and fat, fixing her car's transmission

by sanding moons on the body at night.
Listen to your cousin make beats
and let his sister teach you the "Dougie"

while their mother juggles meth and late rent fees.
Accept it. There is knife throwing with your uncles.
Children run the streets yelling while you drink soda

from a straw in a sandwich bag, and watch
morning jump through a flaming hoop
to avoid the insult of a whip. Afternoon

stands on her hind legs and opens wide, showing
missing teeth. Accept that night stays in his cage.
Remember all that you see. Memory is a fist to the eye.

3.

Some run away with the circus;
I ran away with the canyon,
where there were no tomatoes.

Nothing suns the canyon floor
or grows along the freeway but trash,

no overgrowth of eucalyptus and elm,
frayed palm trees, or mangled brush
to shade the snagging of teenager's

bruised lips in braces. No secret trail
leads to foyers and dens furnished
with broken box springs and books

without tables. This beach
of rocks is where furniture
and mattresses swim to die.

Freeway on one side, backyards treed
with barbeques and sheds on the other,
the canyon flourishes with cenotaphs

of reddened tin and grey wood.
With nothing but time, crops
of bottles and chicken bones,

thrown from the freeway,
stretch   upward   restlessly
in the six by nine of sun.

4.

When ice cream was
the only bribe needed

to tell my grandmother
my cousins walked
the canyons to meet
with their boyfriends,

I should have asked
for a soda, too.

When I leaned against a fence,
playing with a chicken bone
breaking with cracks from the sun,

when only me and a recliner's bones
or the bleached skull of a plastic bag

could be seen, I could've
panted in some heat, too.

At nine, I had no language for lonely,
but could watch cars swim laps forever.

The fence shared a common tongue,
but had no place to go,

if it no longer liked where
it lived, could not move

to my neighborhood,
where we were
racist neighbors,

suspicious of strange fences,
where cars piled in our dirt yard,

and no one listened to the pink
seat of a swing as it licked
the ground with only one chain.

5.

I was two
in a ruffled blue tuxedo

when Donna Thomas
and David Martinez
exchanged vows
and traded rings.

In a decade
their marriage misfired,

their hearts stopped
spinning and roses
rising from vases
slouched.

My grandmother grew
roses and cactus

on the side of her house;
in a front yard of dirt
grew half-sanded cars
blooming with Bondo.

On the porch,
I listened to my grandfather
sing in a rusted tongue.

His sharpest tool was tomorrow.

The ice cream man's song
was my jam;

I'd jump the low,
leaning fence surrounding the yard,
slapping the light pole as I went by.

At night, young men
huddled under the yellow light,
their pants sagging,

their homemade tattoos
thickening with age.

I laughed at how
their underwear in jowls
hung past their belt,
at the broken belt loops
toothed with dirt.

Me and my primas played
under the kitchen light,

our bodies bumping against the table,
tipping the chilies and spilling the salt.

Outside, blue and red rotated
on the sheet over the window,
the tied ends on the curtain rod

flickered like Christmas
while cruisers converged

and black men ran and slid
across hoods. When
everyone was braceleted,

cops talked into their shoulders
in squawks and pauses,

picked up the spilled pockets
and tipped-over bottles,

laughing as they nudged
the boys against
the hoods of their cars.

6.

I shall wear my Chuck Taylors
        beige guts aglow,

crease my khakis
        to a sharp shank.

I will swing first
        or shoot my mouth

at any tremble
        of trouble.

A bandana grows
        from the soiled edges

of my right pocket. Look how
        it grows. Look.

When the moon slicks the night
        motherly, me and my boys nibble

our beer bottles. And know
        the slant of pride, the hubris

of a first tattoo: walking shirt off, chest out,
        the edges raised on a fresh brocade of name.

And my family didn't recognize pride:
        being a father before seventeen,

running in a black gang, and
        losing my tongue— burying it in the dirt of our yard.

When brought home in the back of cruisers,
        lights let the neighbors in—on what was up.

7.

Tonight I can write the most violent lines,

maim the beautiful, misprision the sublime,
decapitate rhyme with chiming execution,

kidnap with the prolonged rip and break of poems;
tonight, in the rain, in anger, I violence lines.

Write, for example, the eyes are starry,
when fists blue and shiver off the distance.

The night, in anger, scratches out the sky.
On a night like this, on a hospital bed, I squinted
under the upmost light, stitched and stitched again,

a stethoscope swayed in the ventilated air.
I scratched the air trying to chase it away.
Tonight I write from a foxhole of hate.

To think I have slipped in this docile skin.
The sounds fall in from the street, chased in.

What does it matter the night has healed,
a scar shines in the sky, a scar shines on my head.

That is all. The night is filled with holes.
I rifle my memory, nothing but

the same light whitening my head;
the art of shame so short and healing so long.

I don't love them anymore, that's certain, but how I loved them;
so much, my fists tried to ride the wind from their teeth.

On nights like this, I too, made women
mountains to climb, flowers to pick, giants to nuzzle

but, I too, have seen my grandmother wrinkled
with realization, white tears falling from

the lines of her face and her unpinned hair,
how all she could do was chop onions

when love and silently turning the cheek
couldn't stop uncles from touching nieces.

8.

As a boy I died
into silent manhood.

I hid the words
teachers helped me find.

People always pine for the ease
of an earlier time, when life

was lunch-boxed with fruit
in the water fountain line,

so much explained during recess time.
I hid the words teachers helped me find.

I spoke in the twist
of fingers to gang signs.

In the color of shoe laces
or which way my brim was tilt,

I hid the words teachers
helped me find.

9.

At nine
years old

I sat in
understudy

at the bar,
worshiping

Shirley Temples.
Grandpa smiled

and said
Let's go

as I chewed
a maraschino,

Dante's devil,
a cherry

in nine
rings of ice.

I finished
the meat,

threw down
the stem.

I laughed,
enjoying

the tart tingle
of grandpa's

old,
red bones

teetering
in beer.

10.

The old man's
shine box is

impotent
without him.

Nothing can be

long in our
belongings.

What's ours
loses what

we are

as the word
life

lost
from

its Latin
root,

celibacy.

Death
unsexes

possessions.

11.

When I was

quick to whoop

a motherfucker's ass

sleeping was tough.

I dreamed of sleeping

perfectly still—

a macho's rest;

muggers, murderers, and fathers

curled up,

sucking sleep's thumb.

II

TO THE YOUNG

black male dressed
like a punk rock

hipster club kid
with teddy bears

tied to his sneakers:
you too are split

down the middle,
like your mother,

bent in front
of the kitchen table

with New Edition
in the background

for three hours
as she sews your gray

and pink acid wash
jeans at the crotch

to make a new,
mixed breed.

Only Chicano rockers
moshing in a corner

with leather jackets
and skin head pins,

and white boys
banging Crip

with dirty blonde corn
rows held with gel

can know
your pain.

And their mothers,
too.

SHED

In the wood shed
I found my uncle's magazines.

Snooping out of boredom,
looking for a wrench
to loosen a question in my body,

I flipped along glossy women
in kitchens without sinks
and refrigerators without food,
where bored housewives released
frustrations by
fucking the plumber,

where gardeners were pulled into pool houses
by college freshmen, their pig tails
doing most of the raking;
I saw women and horses
and women and circles of men
and women and women.

There seemed to be no shortage of women.

Being eleven with the drain pulled
on my wondered lust, my eyes
began to see sex everywhere,

in the plunging of stopped toilets,
in gas tanks being filled, in the pool halls
where my father circled his cue.

How the world moaned and pumped,
and hope flashed fluorescently through the blinds.

I lost my virginity three years later
to a girl without a name,
a neighbor in my curiosity about the body.

Before we did it, she said,
I don't make sounds during sex
and she didn't, just waited blankly,
waited to have emotion scribbled on her.

Eventually, love marked me
with a woman who walked with tumultuous hips—
she made bathrooms and classrooms more exciting,

and proved old Walt right— the body does
electric— when a kiss jumps the body—

as love is the leap of moment suspended
between jumping and landing, learning
and knowing, quitting and starting again

and it hurts more than just in skin
to walk because your walked away from,
and no hurt scatters, no love vanishes,
and no sorrow dissipates or forgives,
and no words can be eaten.
Nothing can be eaten.

And her climbing up a balcony on the second
floor to break in through the sliding glass door
to leave, on a puffed pillow, music she made for you

wont screw back together what was shed.
No one wants to leave the comfort of wood,
or finally say goodnight. I wish the world
had left me cuddled with boxes and magazines,

with boxed wine and videos of Vegas.
Can another cigarette break keep
the shell of sleep from cracking,

stay the flashes of her bent under another man?
Wondering if she is across the country, or the street,
how can I stop her monuments, not hear her again?

SABBATH FE MINUS

The word *weekend*
must come from *weaken*,
long estranged from *wedded*,
from the language of late bars
and early living rooms,

originally meaning,
before distortion,
to have fun.

So many of my Saturday mornings
are closed blinds, rolling over more sleep.

If not for Sunday barbeques after basketball
we would surely honor the Sabbath;
me, and the brothers I ball with,
call when there are two bat swings
and a baby's breath of trouble.

Our sports have bats, engines, or darts;
our favorite games are ones with balls,
ones where the object is to score
through an ancient triangle, box, or hole.

The Mayans put to death the winners of their games;
but none of my boys have been sacrificed,
and Sundays are less prayer
than fights with strangers running
to their cars to pull their pistols.

On Sunday, on the sidelines of the gym,
I dribble and talk, flick ears and slap box,
and look at the rim and at its height—
so large and familial.

Because we are a family of weekends
weakened by drinking and weed
and women in cell phone pictures
with their heads truncated,
but bodies round and supple.

And we are weak in the knees
when our boy talks about Sabertooth
in the back of his truck—Sabertooth
a woman with a beautiful face
and a beautiful body,
but with teeth like a wildcat.

And she is a wild cat in the red boot of our dreams.

But I am quiet because I have no stories;
my boys are laughing and say I care too much,
that I have grown round and supple,
they ask when am I due with her baby.

I laugh because it's funny and because it's true.
I reached into the box of my chest
and found the ball of my heart.

My homeboys will go out but I am going home
and I know, like me, eventually they will go home
and when those prodigal boyfriends return,

they will climb in to bed, like me, and
wrap their arms around a stranger waist.
The wings of our shoulder blades collectively

stretching and extending over bright amens.

CALIFORNIA PENAL CODE 266

On the blade
he glides behind his bitch,
a white tee set sail
on the rolling concrete walk.

Cautious of sirens and lights,
submerged in alleys,
undulating over park grass,
he avoids the walkie-talkies'
antennae in the dark.

In the eighties he break danced,
in the nineties he banged,

now he stands in front of a mirror
working on fresh gestures:

the chain toss
the watch snap
the collar pop.

He's had thirty names;
they collect like barnacles
on his crisp white hull.

In his silence he always
has something to say.

On the blade, the strip, the track,
shiny cars nudge through the streets,
weaving wakes of paint.

Navigating the night
by the brim of his baseball hat,
only with the gust of a few thighs.

His lax tongue blows full,
only by a john's desires
does he stay afloat.

IN CHICANO PARK

No matter if half the park is concrete
and stanchions supporting a bridge,

near industrial buildings yellow in the sun,
their stalks of smoke soaring awake,

next to empty lots and bus stops
without seats or signs or schedules,

near houses bright with paint
the color of dented cans of Spam,

men walking the streets to work
look longingly towards their doors.

No matter if all the murals decay
and the statue of Zapata falls,

more months pile to be swept, and years
ironed, folded, and put away in drawers,

and if jail bars bite off chunks of your view,
remember a wise gambler's words on craps:

call for the dice back. And between rolls,
wipe the dust off the dice, as bills coil a foot

in the wind because life is a wild emotion
lying in the grass, soon to be green.

Not even bags of chips, cheetahs with wind,
avoid being tackled, gouged, and ripped apart.

We all eventually submit, are arched over
by a hyena grin and growl in the sun.

Soon the spots will show and the world will pull tight with relief
as the jungle rallies around us, as we smile now and cry later.

THE ONLY MEXICAN

The only Mexican that ever was Mexican, fought in the revolution
and drank nightly, and like all machos, crawled into work crudo,

letting his breath twirl, then clap and sing before sandpaper
juiced the metal. The only Mexican to never sit in a Catholic pew

was born on Halloween, and ate his lunch wrapped in foil against
the fence with the other Mexicans. They fixed old Fords where my

grandfather worked for years, him and the welder Juan wagered
each year on who would return first to the Yucatan. Neither did.

When my aunts leave, my dad paces the living room and then rests,
like a jaguar who once drank rain off the leaves of Cecropia trees,

but now caged, bends his paw on a speaker to watch crowds pass.
He asks me to watch grandpa, which means, for the day; in town

for two weeks, I have tried my best to avoid this. Many times he will swear,
and many times grandpa will ask to get in and out of bed, want a sweater,

he will ask the time, he will use the toilet, frequently ask for beer,
about dinner, when the Padres play, por que no novelas, about bed.

He will ask about his house, grandma, to sit outside, he will question
while answering, he will smirk, he will invent languages while tucked in bed.

He will bump the table, tap the couch, he will lose his slipper, wedging it in
the wheel of his chair, like a small child trapped in a well, everyone will care.

He will cry without tears—a broken carburetor of sobs. When I speak Spanish, he shakes his head, and reminds me, he is the only Mexican.

INNOMINATUS

Nothing is more nomadic than names,

especially handles given by friends: Slim
because we are thin or because of a haircut, Skullet.

And who knows us less than parents,
givers of our government names—

when my father's tongue axed the air,
my pants fell down from the roar of his belt.

And so, Sundays become shibboleths,

and I watch football,
with three friends disloyal to the town—

a town, that sober or drunk, would put a foot to their throat—

and after a commercial where a boy at school runs
from his parents, fogies wearing spangled pants and mullets,
I ask my friends if they would shy from their father.

Silence makes us explain ourselves.

Before I finish bottling my question,
they wish.

They wish the motherfucker
was there—in a thong, a tutu, in more makeup than RuPaul,
picking them up from school, as long as they knew him.
And I know these three men are lying,
each of us sitting one cushion removed on the couch.

Just because you and your dad share the same name
and you live under his protective hand,
doesn't mean it protects,

when the only time he picks you up from school,
the locks open in gossip
when he chases you through the halls,

through the football field,
and into a canyon.

Bushes can be the warmest blanket.

Is there a way to explain over football and beer,
your father's childhood was a contortionist's dream.

When the radio station signed off,
grandfather kept drinking mescal and singing.

When the bottle swallowed his tongue,

like the small segmented worm our tongues are,
the man spoke the language he knew well,

spelled what his illiterate fist could form.
The letters passed from generation to generation;

a nepotism from fathers, from mothers:
violence is the oldest inheritance:

Given for the first lie, the first blow, the first scam in a back seat,
the first laugh, the first time you are left alone and crying,
the first to say I told you so, the first man to fall charging the hill.

Because it is the test of words and not the word that endures,
because the moon toils toward the forever foot print

the bible should be revised and the list
of who begot whom should include Neil Armstrong.

And homegirls, you should know,
before an alpha, before the first word or a god
there was a riot of silence to be banded and named.

Every person, animal, and willow should waver in a whisper
is not in the bible, but it should be.

It should be, because, homeboy,
you came home and your mother was in the kitchen
cooking and the records spun on their axis
and your life was a flower to dance around her

or your mother was on the couch drunk,
stumbling to get up off her slur,
and your life was a flower to dance around her,

taunting her to fill the silence with a name, any name.

III

MOTION AND REST

A bird picking twigs and stray paper would seem to be safest in motion, stasis being the natural precursor of stagnation and death. But this Spring I have seen two yellow birds picked while in motion. A bird poked the grass for food when a cat in full acceleration and leap, pawed it out of flight. A week later, during a break between classes, I reconciled with a woman on the phone. Another bird skittered among the branches. I made a big show of insinuating to the woman that she had competition, when a falcon swooped and clutched the bird in its talons only five feet away from me. I could only continue to talk on the phone; genteelly remarking, with no shortage of smiled pride, how commensurately tenuous life is for the dancing cautious and those stricken with motion.

•

The only animals I saw growing up were pigeons. These ubiquitous little hipsters, their mismatched feathers and congregating ways, are rarely targets of predators. Besides the danger of unsuspecting cars, pellet guns, or bored teenage boys with Alka-Seltzer, pigeons amble the streets of San Diego. Their necks wiggle when they walk. In Houston, the circle of life is much more evident. I share my yard with cats and dogs, blue jays, cardinals, owls, with possums, squirrels, mosquitoes, cicadas, and cockroaches. They are the autochthonous residents; we have come to a silent truce. And that is the paradox: in San Diego, I was more scared of a car driving through the neighborhood. I was quicker to violence, didn't think twice about putting a shoe on a spider. In Houston, I have only seen the violence of nature. I have new fears. I am more scared of a possum's eyes and tail, of walking to the grocery store and being bitten by a stray.

•

My father spoke in tongues, never wore clothes with peace signs because my mother took the symbol for broken crosses, and I spent each Halloween dressed as a wise man with a bathrobe for a thawb and a dishtowel and sweatband for a keffiyah; and despite this childhood, I have never worn my parents' notion of a spiritual world or an after life. Dreams can mature in to belief. After a nightmare about a former girlfriend, I felt the urge to do laundry. In Houston, oak trees canopy the streets, and the concrete has been uprooted by hurricanes and heat. The sidewalks and driveways are cracked, as is the laundry room floor in my garage apartment. I live on a corner lot where once a house stood. Missing things hide. In my apartment, when the wind blows, it shakes, and when I walk, it speaks. How the garage apartment came to have no accompanying home, how it lost guidance, I have no idea, but I believe the house was smote from the earth.

•

The legend goes like this: it was a dreary morning. The house slept but the renter lay awake, shivering in his own fears. Love had pulled up her hair. Climbing out of bed sweaty, he sorted clothes. Colors with colors and whites with whites was the only way to separate his situation. Isn't that how we learn? Everything in its box and everything in its proper time. The whites must be washed first, bleach was the order he sought. So out with his blue plastic basket he creaked across his bedroom to the living room and down the stairs, unlocked the laundry room deadbolt and turned the handle. Now I must explain: the renter was not a religious man, but his mother had always felt deep within her bones that he was a prophet. He was named after his father and her favorite bible character. Upon his arrival at adulthood, she was mightily disappointed, but still handed him a set of keys to her house, and showed him where the paperwork was hidden. So when the rapture comes, he should get what he could for her home. She was pious. Her husband was pious. Frogs are pious. But the renter was not pious because when he opened the door six frogs waited at the cracks in his laundry room floor, their throats flooded with croaks, swallowing him whole. In moments of judgment, all things are possible, frogs ride on the back of concrete cracked by scales, only to slowly, without turning, ease back into the earth, one croak at a time, as the house did, leaving only a garage apartment.

•

Often, the most ordinary fears obscure the most obvious truths. The frogs of the apocalypse visit me. When I spoke again to the woman who wouldn't reconcile, I told her about the two birds, she said it was a sign. Her accent lingers on the phone's receiver, pitches phosphor and smoke. When I was younger, and cars with killed headlights sped through our neighborhood and if no one was shot, the first question was, what sign did they throw up? The world brims with signs. We feel the ineffable movement of the frock of god never far from our actions yet we are never near the actions of gods. Escalators are the most honest *deus ex machinas*; in their thawed stillness, in their motion and rest, they capture paradox. My life is an escalator of hiding my stinger from my own apocalypse. Everyday I cross from silence into speech. Every day trickles of people whisper over the border with their children *or for their children*, like Nicodemus they believe they must reenter the womb. On the interstates and roads with the heaviest traffic of illegal immigrant crossing, the silhouette of a family running is posted; like the signs for crossing deer, they show us the hunt. Show us which signs to climb. Tell us to wait for heaven; to run the world from the kitchen and back lawn, or for husbands to speed ahead and let go of their wives, forget the child. To take the proper shape. To tell us the color of caution. To tell us the last American exit. To show the rest of us the free way.

SMALL DISCOVERIES

Sometimes I count the animals I'm not,
catalogue the ways I'm not covered in spots

or will never struggle up heated bark
to branches extended over yellowed grass.

It's nice to add up the ways my antlers
will never itch, my pouch wont carry a joey,

wont feast on parasites off a shark's skin, nor will I
be pushed out of a tree and expected to fly,

why would I ever make a nest in the walls
of someone's home: In which I discover

in scraps of pillow fillings and bits of paper
that the Amazon will wither away in a decade.

I discover, turtles live on every continent except
Antarctica, in any climate they can lock shells

and mate. I discover unicorns shall come down,
and the bullock with their bulls; and their land

shall be soaked with blood, and their dust made fat
with fatness. The throne of Denmark is made from

the bones of unicorns. My childhood is a unicorn;
no, my childhood is a form of taxidermy, of dust,

a kind of myth made in this monkey shack
of skin, where the price of sophistication

is to roll over and expose the tender
underbelly of learning how to play dead.

THE SOFA KING

With a dynasty of furniture
he breaks pipes

and pushes down cushions
while gaming.

How he does it,
no one knows.

His people
eat pizza,

excited as a rule,
breaking into perspiration,

as the cheese genuflects
in staggered curtsies,

and the smell makes one
gesture: a flick of the thumb,

and swords splish down
and tigers lift out

and night breaks against
one mother without—

Sofa king be smart in a crown of smoke.
Sofa king be stupid, you pill popping animal.

APOTROPAIC

I agree with Sigmund,
sex is like air,
but it's also like

a sea monster summoned
by scared people
with a virgin chained
to a sacrificial stone.

We all slay.

In middle school, one morning,
I noticed my mother was a woman
while she put on her nylons.

She knew by my eyes,
as all women know by eyes,
I had left her hip.

Because my father always spoke
and my mother lacked a smile,
I ignored them both.

Having given up
pleasing my father
and loving my mother

I started playing
"Clash of the Titans."

In my room alone,
pretending to be Perseus
I followed Athena's owl,
and killed Poseidon's kraken—

I laid down Medusa
without looking in her eyes.

Sigmund also said,
that Medusa with her head of cocks
castrates the tribe of men—
one look at her and you're hard,
hard as a rock.

And isn't that what men are?
Heavy balls and heavier heads.
Scared limp of origins.

To be mad at women,
women to be mad,
mad to be women,

is the way of the metal, guarded,
shield of the sun.

THE COST OF IT ALL

Trade is the buckle of this world's belt, shiny with dollar signs.

And I know Tibetan windstorms necklace the waking bodies of San Diego.
And I know why Muhammad Ali stood over Sonny Liston flexing.
And I know as we age our tongues grow numb from lying.
And I know in a biblical sense the gust of a humid afternoon.
And I know in chronological and alphabetical order, nothing.
And I know riding in an elevator is a close as one can get to the present.
And I know devotion and honor flicker in Atlanta strip clubs.
And I know why the Chevy Nova couldn't sell in Mejico.

Moon beams of finely threaded rope sway
in the wind. At their end, price tags.

But I wish John Lennon was born with Ringo's nose.
And I wish there were more virgins for me to find and report.
And I wish when she called, the phone protected me.
And I wish every time the moon three-point turns in the asphalt night.
And I wish on continental spots of leopards that California broke into the sea.
And I wish Che's face symbolized more than pimpled years of angst.
And I wish upon a pan with a skiing square of butter headed for steam.
And I wish to tiptoe and hear over the fence of my own teeth.

I have tried to figure the cost of it all with lint and paperclips.

REBECCA'S USE

I was twenty-two and no longer news;

Pooh-butts and Gees creased to a cotton shank,
leaning on rusted fences and drooping stoops,
every part of Meadowbrook Apartments,
nodded or gave up the "P" as I passed.

And though I remember the ice cream
dripping down their youth,

the years also clicked up their wrists,

and the young boys I had known by name,
known by their embarrassing moments,
known by their relation of blood,
now I didn't know what they were called.

But I know what they are.

The boys in the 'Brook
are a jagged apparatus in a jaw,
cutting until pushed out,
replaced by endless rows of teeth.

I made a necklace
of these teeth

and a ring of Rebecca.

Nightly I snuck in her window
cold with beer,
hoping her father didn't hear.

Rebecca was chilled with youth

and I was hard with it;
without a sound we were
instruments of springs and clenched skin,
joint in our body's tool.

Rebecca still in the 'Brook—
belly six months big,
a boyfriend shot in the face,
a little sister all grown up
and staring at me—

pushed me
into the same bunk bed
I'd been hustled in and hid
at night when we were teens.

When she walked, I followed.
In her room, we touched

with precise, machine lust;
we tasted of lime and rust.

I sailed from Rebecca, the 'Brook,

stepping on the serrated edges of my pants,
leaving for a sea of dungarees and chevrons,

a Navy of brooms twirled before being used,
in everything being used.

COVERALLS

The orange coveralls flamed around me in one-size-fits-all,
and no matter how I stood, they slouched and bent me.

In the shipyard there were no mirrors
but in the ocean's reflection or the pools in the dry docks
I could see how the leathers covered my boney clavicle
and my arms were only as wide as my torch.

I interviewed in a flower-splattered rayon,
but was hired because my uncle was foreman.

In training, I met Lucy.

Straightening out the crooked cuts in my bulkheads
she showed me how an orange stream pours off a perfect bevel.

Once in the bilges, I asked what brought her
to the bottom of this boat, measuring and cutting walls.

Pulling off her suede glove,

wiping sweat and ash away,
on her hand shone a green 13.

Secretaries don't have tattoos,
muffled through her respirator.

And by lunch,
we were burnt by sparks,
by three we sneezed black,

but the foreman flirted with her
using the last banging mallets
to get close and whisper.

Wrenching hoses
from our torches,
on our neck, metallic dust
ignited in the sun.

The top half
of her coveralls,
unbuttoned and wrapped,
slowly melted down
as the whistles blew.

After training,
I worked on frigates,
she worked on tankers,

I walked by her worksite
and Lucy'd be cutting
a tanker's wall,

golden ashes
dropping from
a chariot
of rusted pipe
and planks.

Looking up
shaking the wind,

shaking a hole
in my coveralls,

from ankle to knee gone,
the thin blue cloth gone;

I watched Lucy rise.

IV

FORGETTING WILLIE JAMES JONES

1.

It's not water to wine to swallow harm,
though many of us have,

and changing the name
of Ozark Street to Willie Jones Street,
won't resuscitate,

won't expose how the sun roars across rows of faces
at the funeral for a seventeen-year-old boy,

won't stop the double slapping
of the screen door against a frame,
causing a grandmother, by habit, to yell out, *Willie.*

It can't deafen the trophies in a dead teenager's room.
That day in '94 I felt strong.

I walked down the street with nickel bags of weed
in the belt loops of my Dickies,

and a bandana strung from my pocket.

That's when I thought trouble could be run from,
could be avoided by never sitting
with your back to the door
or near a window.

I swore by long days and strutted along a rusted past,
shook dice and smoked with the boys

that posted on the corners:
and men cruising in coupes, men built so big
they took up both seats,
I rode with them that summer.

That was the season death walked alongside us all,
wagging its haunches and twisting its collared neck
at a bird glittering along a branch.

Willie was shot in that heat,
with a stolen pistol,
in the front yard of a party.

It poked a hole
no bigger than a pebble
in his body.

The shooters came from my high school:
we sometimes smoked in the bungalow
bathrooms during lunch.

A few weeks before Willie got shot,
Maurice had been killed—

An awning after rain,
Maurice and Willie
sagged from the weight.

Some say it is better
to be carried by six
than judged by twelve.

Some say the summer of '94
in Southeast San Diego
was just another summer.

2.

Willie was a little man, barely a man, when he bled out in the grass strewn
  with cups and paper plates sliced with pink frosting.
I recollect on the day Willie was shot and remember nothing. The next day
  in math, when I was told he was dead it meant even less;
nor did it mean much later that day, while I slapped dominoes on their backs

and kept score on a piece of butcher paper with a golf pencil. Circles
  and crosses won nothing. I was a real nihilist that summer,
star of my own show in which I did nothing but smoke menthols and practice
  blowing rings of smoke, a trick I never learned, but I did
learn how to stop a forty ounce of malt liquor from foaming out of the bottle,

drink it fast. I also learned that sitting too long on the two-foot cedar
  block wall in front of Alonzo's house rolling a joint
and balancing your butt so it didn't fall in the hole and rip your pants
  was a quick way of getting punched in the chest by
an older homie who was drunk because he just got out after doing three

years standing on his head, and while you rubbed your chest he would put his arm
  around you and remind you every three minutes he had
walked the yard with the big homies so now he was a big homie, and if you ever
  wanted to be a big homie too, you should punch that poo-butt
bitch in the mouth, without ever explaining who that poo-butt bitch was or what

that poo-butt bitch did. But most of life was like that then, not to be questioned
  or reasoned, so when my baby's mama paged me, I called,
but it was only about bringing formula for my son, whenever I got back, which
  wouldn't be anytime soon, and she knew not to ask when
or where I was, but she would know by the way I smoothed crinkled dollars

on the edge of the table that I had got hot on the dice, or that I had got a few
        good hands playing spades and collected all the books
even though I never had the patience for math, but maybe that's why when
        I finally decide to go home and I stopped at the store for
diapers or wipes, I never reached in my pocket and counted change, or paid.

3.

The most
successful men

I know
whale the halls

for secretaries,
or maybe it just seems

that with an open
mouth and no teeth
they feed.

Nom nom nom
on the living.

Nom nom
on the dead.

Giving
brain

is slang
for fellatio.

How hilarious,
"ha-ha"

of nature
that

black widow
spiders,

ravenous
with

red
hourglass,

instruct their mate
by mouth.

4.

My aunt spoke
of the day

JFK
was assassinated

with a reverence
she saved

for the pope
or Joe Montana.

She loved Joe Montana.
I hated the '9ers

and Golden Joe, too.
She loved to say:

Only great people
are assassinated,

and these gangsters
out here getting

smoked ain't great,
just fools,

and every fool
dies.

5.

Tupac finally turned off
the life he left on
in an empty Vegas street,

but he was always a winner
around my block where people got shot,

and not just once
but were repeat champions
of almost winning in life.

When we heard about Tupac's murder,
we soccered in conversation,
a few wearing shirts with his face.

We stole liquor in honor
of him, and with cigarettes bouncing
like diving boards

hinged on a spring in our mouths,
we lit a large "P"
in the street and poured
more booze each time the flame died down.

Sitting with E.Y. on the curb, passing a joint,
he told me he wished he had played hockey,

that too many played football, that too many
played basketball, all of us rapped and sold weed,

that too many of us had the same hustle,
and that all of us at some point would sit in a cell

and play spades while someone braided our hair,
that he could have showed them white boys something.

In three years he would be killed in crossfire
in San Francisco,
after getting up twice from being shot
in San Diego.

6.

Some things we find in the dirt,
some in the Appalachians, some
in the early morning swirl
of scientists working on the big secrets,

where they unearth wads of frozen tobacco
and rub together broken wagon wheels
to understand the romance settlers had with spruces.

All that without quizzing the trees. All without figuring
a seed can only be grown towards, grabbed with the right soil and rain.
Most of my best years rubbed together truths

and secret lies. In hospital wards, men pucker
at vending machines, children surround squirrels with prisons
of juice boxes; neither feel the needle of breathing fruitless dreams.
At the zoo, young lovers kiss while a chewing giraffe watches.

In my bag, I find Juicy Fruit with a skin of sticky silver.
At the beach, tourists pull their edentulous dreams.
Like lipstick on a collar, a ring of steam on a coffee table.

Some, with great hubris, believe Texas
to be the most natural state based on size and shape.
Some things we find in the dirt that weren't there before.

We were both the slightest of people, Willie and I;
Maurice was a bigger man and younger;
women clutched their purses and picked up their dogs at him.
No one waits by a window, pinching their arm, waiting for him.

7.

Teenagers stare at the storm of clouds on my arms;
they loll for hours on the grass and dream.

I too have stared at weathered tattoos, and wished.
In the summer of '94, three-finger rings on each hand was the world's prize,

the largest debate was which malt liquor to buy with two dollars,
'94 was also a pigeon's cochineal throat cooing inside cupped hands;
but especially, was the backs of house shoes folded under heels.

My closest homie spoke of his woman
the way some spoke of their Impalas:
her teeth were the color of baking soda
and cocaine boiling in a mayonnaise jar,

the black-bottomed pot tilting on the hot rose of the stove,
as a child wearing only a diaper peers over a tricycle's handlebars.

In the necropolis of that summer, sirens ambulanced
the streets toward more victims.

Gangster Ern was killed during a home invasion.
Bubba Cheeks was hit four times while driving.
Maurice was run down on his bike as get-back.
Willie Jones was slumped in retaliation for that.

I wanted so badly to go to prison,
wanted my stripes and the respect of teens,
wished I had been in the car that drove by
and dumped death and sickle
in the yard of Willie's graduation party.

I went to Maurice's funeral
with a shaved head
and a black barrette
on my rat tail.

At the casket, I reached in my pocket for
a bullet to place in his hidden death suit.

Between the preacher's clapping and hopping, he pointed at our four rows,
the church turned and shook their heads in unison.

Afterward, our circle of teenagers and young men spoke
of retaliations and getbacks, drive-bys and screwdrivers.
I stood silently, stabbing myself with a menthol.

8.

Just as Perseus raised his bag,
I have held a quarter ounce of weed.

1994 is a coal in the stocking of my stomach;
there is no hope it can be pressed into a diamond.

In Houston, so educated now, I cock my honor.
For instance: Little T.K. shot himself in the front yard

of his girlfriend's house with a pistol he stole
from his brother's underwear drawer.

Or Albert from Emerald Hills, locked up
somewhere down south on a gun charge

could somersault the entirety of our block
without a single tumble or scratch.

Little Eight has been shot six times;
and once, in a room with Rebecca,

I held the door closed with one leg, naked,
while she held tight under my body

with her arms and legs and asked me
to never let anyone touch her

because my homies pushed against the door
of Carlito's spare bedroom without a bed

and whispered to let them watch, let them shoot video.
How strong I felt in '94, when the most chivalrous

thing I could do was block a door,
stop a rape.

OF MOCKINGBIRDS

By my roofs and poles

a few murders
of crows occurred.

With the forensics of feet
pigeons investigate

the scene, chalking
an outline of feathers,

analyzing splatter
patterns of trash.

The wind moans longingly;

there is no evidence
of tomorrow.

Burgles of cats
scratch a furniture
of cloud and night air;

dogs, loose from packs,
butts put out on the ground,
roll over in the gutters,

and a mockingbird,
darkening a drag of wires,

croons a tune from his
pompadour and beak.

A freestyle from the beat
of leaves and trees,

away from the origins
of the bird's own tongue,

he beeps, whistles, and chimes.
In this mickey fickey of sagged

pants and homemade tattoos,
the haggard muse
tickles his beautiful black ear

with a car's alarm.

SCIENTIFICALLY SPEAKING

There have
been exciting

discoveries
in the field

of me.
Many

of which,
I have

made
myself.

THIS BIRD CHEST HOLDS A BIRD'S HEART

On our birch wood bed,
She was crying in chirps
when I entered in her underwear.

I couldn't fill them the way she did,
or shimmy while putting on my jeans,
the bright embroidery peacocking light.

She's a woman who
knows where the sea goes
without seeing its edge.

The kicking of her feet
makes the splayed sheets shake
when she wakes and tests the air.

She loves in secret with her socks.

In her intricate answers:
Beauty is never simple.
Beauty is always there.

I wear her underwear to hear her laugh,
a little red bow on the butt to forget,

to fill our little room without a closet,
painted yellow and filled with holes
from a constant rotation of paintings.
To fill it full of us, full of her eyes

and my arms, full of our mothers—young,
laughing at their six year old flapping

in heels, staggering in foolishness.

MIDTERM ANSWERS FOR ENGLISH B

1. If there were one person I could have a drink with, it would be Dali. He partied.

2. For several years now different races blamed other races for the problems they face.

3. All questions can come about reading James Baldwin's "ALL QUESTIONS".

4. Furthermore, superlogical prewised the poststupidity in my metamatrix of ineffability.

5. California is by far the greatest, and I have been to Wyoming, of the 52 states.

6. And that is why the government put us to bed without dinner or a bedtime song.

7. Emily Dickinson should have worn more make-up; she might have liked marriage.

8. He opened me like a can of Coke, Mexican Coke, which can be recycled at corner stores.

9. To Gerard Manley Hopkins, and many other writers, salivation was a gift from God.

10. John Donne understood we have had a war between the sexes since the 1800's.

11. French Surrealists are right, about what I'm unsure, but I am confident they knew.

12. Everyone should watch the movie Anonymous, it shows how stupid Shakespeare was.

13. Thomas Stern only went by T. S. because he was lazy; his glasses scream procrastinator.

14. Whitman was wonderful: the type of man a butterfly or bambi is drawn towards.

15. Since the beginning of time man has used language to communicate.

16. And people still, even in our advanced society, take video games for granite.

17. There will be a day when there are no books, when everything is read with just your eyes.

18. In my mind's eye, the battle for best modern poet is between Lil Wayne and Lady Gaga.

19. *The Great Gatsby* should be handed out in high school kids in the ghetto.

20. Therefore, logically, Martin Luther King is a mass murderer and hypocrite.

21. If I ever met a kid like Holden Caulfield, I would punch him in the nose.

22. If only I could climb myself out from under this grave of papers to grade.

A SUNDAY MARCH

In boot camp we walked to want to—

unlike companies marching one, two,
three and four, their APOC's calling cadence
the way a good sailor would—

—because good squids hospital corners
and much is said about swabies and beds
and much is said about squaring off salutes,

so much time devoted to creasing

dungarees or cleaning latrines
—that marching boots in unison,

once it's gotten;
is almost forgotten.

But Johnson, the blackest man I ever met
with the darkest Georgia accent I ever heard,
called cadence swaying from inside:

heads turned when we marched by.

With Johnson's chest loving the air,
other CC's would stare
and Senior Chief would only smile;

we marched with
our chins high.

But an officer with squared away hair
stopped our company in the street
because he couldn't count the song
or measure the syllables of Johnson's steps.

Screaming about disrespecting drill,
he pulled Johnson by the collar,
how *three-four* correctly said
could possibly sound like read the floor.

In those moments minacity
becomes visible; the full spectrum

colors above our bodies,
as we move over another:

as I have seen men, bloody and full of fear
rainbow over other men,
trying to break the glass of another song.

Beauty can prism power
but once again power buckled beauty.

And Johnson was again just one face of thirty,
one cocked lid swaying against the sunlight.

THE MECHANICS OF MEN

I have never been the most mechanically inclined of men.
      Wrenches, screwdrivers, or shovels
have never made nice with me. In the shipyard,

I worked alone, in the dark, deep in
      the bilges of frigates. For two months,
I hooked a torch to an oxygen tank with a green line and pulled a red

hose through bulkheads to gas. The brass tool
      hissed like an ostrich
when it fed on metal. That day, my flame cut

permanent deck fittings; the loops fell like bright oranges;
      I ripened the rusty metal. I knew
that this was a job to baby-sit me, a job they gave to bad burners,

beginners playing with their tools: who pretended their brass torches
      were trumpets, and that gulls in the bay were tables
of distracted diners. When my father was a boy, his father loaded him

and his siblings in the car and dropped them off downtown
      so my grandfather could get drunk and my
grandmother could pretend he wasn't drinking again. When I was a boy,

I enjoyed watching my father dig; with dirt between his palms, he spun
      the shovel before he dug. As I grew, I tried
to stay away from work, even when he paid me. I stayed away from him too.

I never understood how he could work around so much grass. For him,
      life was work. For him, everything was hard. For me,
it was not hard. He stalked my mother a long time after their divorce.

He never understood she was not sod to be laid, or a sprinkler to be
             attached to a pvc pipe seven inches in the ground.
That pregnant at fifteen was too soon. Neither of us is the most

mechanical of men, yet we still pride ourselves on how we fashion our tools.
             I wake up shivering and crying in an empty bed,
the afternoon light entering and leaving an empty bottle of wine near

an emptier glass—or roll over and try, and fail, to remember a woman's
             name, which never really gets old, just uncouth
to say so, and feel broke. To feel fixed is to feel a mechanical spirit, to feel love,

or at least to play at paste for an evening, to make believe she will never leave me,
             as life almost did when I cut the green hose, and was
lonely and shaking that day on the deck of the destroyer, looking into the

green water, and wondered what would be written on my tomb:
             "Killed by oxygen was this unmechanical man."
In that moment close to death, I only wanted my own lungs. I didn't regret

returning home and sleeping on my father's couch. And that summer, I returned
             to each of the women of my past and bedded
them all, trying to reheat our want. I don't regret that– drinking wine

and making love, or writing poems and making love, of wanting to stay
             but nonetheless leaving. I don't regret returning
with Said and Spivak, with Weil and Augustine, of telling my father

"All sins are an attempt to fill voids," or rebuilding my grandfather's
             house with Hopkins in my head
as I ripped the tar and shingles off the old roof with a shovel.

And I am not mad for being the second favorite son,
       Esau turned inside out. Can't regret saying
that summer, I was, in fact, already, a bigger and better man

than my father because I understood more. I didn't mind he
       favored my younger brother, who knew less
than him. I favored my brother's way of living, of skating

in the park and smoking weed while I studied and wondered for us all.
       How ridiculous I was that summer for us all;
for not attempting to rebuild any of his love that summer, at all.

NOTES

I would like to thank Tony Hoagland, Sandra Alcosser, and Glover Davis for mentoring me.

I would like to thank Kevin Prufer, Ilya Kaminsky, Martha Serpas, and Marilyn Chin for working so diligently with me.

I would like to thank Eduardo C. Corral, Rigoberto Gonzalez, Matt Hart, Mark Irwin, David St. John, Carol Muske-Dukes, Katie Farris, Chris Baron, jay kastely, Mat Johnson, Alex Parsons, Robert Boswell, Antonya Nelson, Ange Mlinko, and Jehrico Brown for giving me important advice, encouragement, or help when I needed it.

I would like to thank the University of Houston, San Diego State University, and CantoMundo for giving me a community of writers to befriend.

I would like to thank Houston Mafia: Karyna McGlynn, Beth Lyons, Justine Post, and Becca Wadlinger for helping me shape up the manuscript in the later stages. Also thank you, J.S.A. Lowe. Extra shout to Karyna for taking a long, bad title and giving back a shorter, better title.

I would like to thank Jenny Minnit-Shippey, Megan Marshall-Joseph, Leigh Pollack, and Lizz Huerta for helping me with early stages of the manuscript.

I would also like to thank all of the people in the CWP's at U of H and SDSU, your friendship has been invaluable. I would also like to thank both English department secretaries and staff, so many times you saved me.

A huge shoutout goes to Sarabande Books; specifically, all love to Sarah Gorham, Jeffrey Skinner, Kirby Gann, Kristin Radtke, Megan Bowden, and the intern Anthony. We made a beautiful book together.

I would like to thank Brian Romero for the cover art and for years of friendship, late nights, and plenty of tattoos.

The biggest thanks goes to my family: Mom, Mark, Dad, Dalila, Jeremiah, David Anthony, Isiah James—and of course, to Brittney Keefer Martinez.

ACKNOWLEDGMENTS

Thanks to the editors of the following journals in which some of these poems, or earlier version of them, first appeared:

Border Voices: "Coveralls"
Caldera Review: "Palomar Mountain"
Charlotte: "Calaveras Part 2"; "Calaveras Part 3"
Drunken Boat: "The Only Mexican"; "Circus, Circus"
Forklift, Ohio: "Innominatus"
Poetry International: "Rebecca's Use"
San Diego Writer's Ink Anthology Volume 2: "This Bird Chest Hold's a Bird's Heart"
San Diego Writer's Ink Anthology Volume 3: "Sabbath Fe Minus"

David Tomas Martinez has been published in *Forklift;
Ohio, Poetry International, Drunken Boat, Caldera
Review,* and has been a featured poet in Border
Voices and NBC Latino. He is a PhD candidate in the
University of Houston's Creative Writing Program in
Poetry. Martinez is also the Reviews and Interviews
Editor for *Gulf Coast: A Journal of Literature and Fine
Arts,* and a CantoMundo Fellow.

Sarabande Books thanks you for the purchase of this book; we do hope you enjoy it! Founded in 1994 as an independent, nonprofit, literary press, Sarabande publishes poetry, short fiction, and literary nonfiction—genres increasingly neglected by commercial publishers. We are committed to producing beautiful, lasting editions that honor exceptional writing, and to keeping those books in print. If you're interested in further reading, take a moment to browse our website, www. sarabandebooks.org. There you'll find information about other titles; opportunities to contribute to the Sarabande mission; and an abundance of supporting materials including audio, video, a lively blog, and our Sarabande in Education program.